SUCKIN HIND TIT
A Book on Religion and Politics
By Dick Grigg, January 2013

MY FAMILY
Parley and Hallie Grigg's 12 living children 1981
Back Row, LR: Golden, Leah, Wells, Eugene, Lamar, Parley
Front Row LR: Dick, Heber, June, James, Kathryn, Nephi (Norma died as infant)

Statue of Liberty, New York Harbor

SUCKIN HIND TIT
A Book on Religion and Politics
By Dick Grigg, January 2013

Sow and pigs

ABOUT THE AUTHOR: He was known as Dick Grigg during his life and fashioned his life according to LDS Church standards, attended college at BYU, University of Utah, College of Idaho, University of California at Berkeley, served a proselytizing mission in California, Family History Mission in Salt Lake City, Utah, and a World Wide Family History Support Mission Remote at home and married twice in an LDS Temple. He has kept a daily journal most of his life and has been the family historian for many years. He has served as a Family History Center Director and Family History Consultant for many years. He has researched and cleared thousands of family names for the temple and conducted family temple excursions to do these names. He and his wife Angie have been family name extractors and indexers since 1983 for the LDS Church. They extracted and cleared the names of Hernando Cortes and the conquistadores who conquered Mexico in 1521. They also identified the Aztec Nobility who were conquered and did their temple work for them. Mr. Grigg has written numerous lessons and documents that are published on the LDS Church's Find Answers data base in the Help Center of the New Family Search program.

ABOUT THIS BOOK: This book is about religion and politics. Our country was founded and established by people who had a deep belief in God because many of them came here specifically to find religious freedom. I believe that God is at the helm and has a hand in what happens to America.

CONTENTS

A Book on Religion and Politics

By Dick Grigg, January 2013

A NOTE ON DICK AND THIS BOOK: I was raised as the youngest of 13 children on farms in Southern Idaho and Eastern Oregon. I remember selling grown pigs for two dollars each and milk cows for ten dollars each. Never the less my dad kept pigs and I fed them. One big sow pig had a litter of 13 little ones and she only had ten tits. There are always those that get in there first and get the good tits (I call them hogs) and the others take the hind tits or have to wait for next time. The hind tits don 't produce as good so the pigs that have to take the hind tits don't grow and thrive as good. The hind titters are stinted in their growth and are called runts because they never grow and gain weight like the hogs do.

I compare this with the United States as being the big sow pig and all the foreign countries we give aid to as little sucking pigs. There just aren't enough tits to satisfy all the wants and needs and our milk is fast drying up. We are to a point now where other countries like China and Russia are the big sow pigs and we are sucking hind tit.

THIS BOOK IS WRITTEN FROM MEMORY: There are no notes or references to look up. It is all experiences of a life time of living with a large family on a farm, going to school, getting on my own with my own family, making a living, living through many political campaigns, several wars and being grandpa and great grandpa.

POLITICS AND RELIGION: I was raised as a Democrat because Roosevelt got the young people working and helped the poor farmers finance their farms and operate them. I went Republican when the Democrats supported abortion.
I was raised to believe in God as the creator of all things both in heaven and on earth through his son, Jesus Christ, the Redeemer and Savior. Also the Holy Ghost or Holy Spirit, a communicator from God to us, to guide us here on earth.
Politics and Religion cannot be separated because politics determines how people are governed on earth. Who wants a leader who denies the one who created him and the Holy Spirit who is given to direct him. A good leader must have faith, hope and charity and the greatest of these is charity. Charity is the pure love of Christ.

CHAPTER 1

Religion and Family

GOD, JESUS AND THE HOLY GHOST: I believe that God through Jesus governs over all, that He has all wisdom, and all power, both in heaven and in earth; and that we cannot comprehend everything which the Lord can comprehend. The reason we are limited in our comprehension here is because we have no memory of life before mortality. This life is a probationary state or trial period where we have the free agency to choose between right and wrong. Every person born into this mortal life is given the ability to know right from wrong. We don't see God while here but He has given us the means by which we can keep in touch with Him through prayer and the administration of the Holy Spirit.

BASIC TEACHINGS OF MY RELIGION
TEN COMMANDMENTS
King James Version

And God spake all these words, saying, I am the Lord thy God, which have brought thee out of the land of Egypt, out of the house of bondage.

1.   Thou shalt have no other gods before me.

2.   Thou shalt not make unto thee any graven image, or any likeness of any thing that is in heaven above, or that is in the earth beneath, or that is in the water under the earth. Thou shalt not bow down thyself to them, nor serve them: for I the Lord thy God am a jealous God, visiting the iniquity of the fathers upon the children unto the third and fourth generation of them that hate me; And shewing mercy unto thousands of them that love me, and keep my commandments.

3.   Thou shalt not take the name of the Lord thy God in vain; for the Lord will not hold him guiltless that taketh his name in vain.

4.   Remember the Sabbath day, to keep it holy. Six days shalt thou labour, and do all thy work: But the seventh day is the sabbath of the Lord thy God: in it thou shalt not do any work, thou, nor thy son, nor thy daughter, thy manservant, nor thy maidservant, nor thy cattle, nor thy stranger that is within thy gates: For in six days the Lord made heaven and earth, the sea, and all that in them is, and rested the seventh day: wherefore the Lord blessed the sabbath day, and hallowed it.

5.   Honour thy father and thy mother: that thy days may be long upon the land which the Lord thy God giveth thee.

6.   Thou shalt not kill.

7.   Thou shalt not commit adultery.

8.   Thou shalt not steal.

9.   Thou shalt not bear false witness against thy neighbour.

10.   Thou shalt not covet thy neighbour's house; thou shalt not covet thy neighbour's wife, nor his manservant, nor his maidservant, nor his ox, nor his ass, nor any thing that is thy neighbour's.

THE ARTICLES OF FAITH
OF THE CHURCH OF JESUS CHRIST OF LATTER-DAY SAINTS
History of the Church, Vol. 4, pp. 535—541

1 WE believe in God, the Eternal Father, and in His Son, Jesus Christ, and in the Holy Ghost.

2 We believe that men will be punished for their own sins, and not for Adam's transgression.

3 We believe that through the Atonement of Christ, all mankind may be saved, by obedience to the laws and ordinances of the Gospel.

4 We believe that the first principles and ordinances of the Gospel are: first, Faith in the Lord Jesus Christ; second, Repentance; third, Baptism by immersion for the remission of sins; fourth, Laying on of hands for the gift of the Holy Ghost.

5 We believe that a man must be called of God, by prophecy, and by the laying on of hands by those who are in authority, to preach the Gospel and administer in the ordinances thereof.

6 We believe in the same organization that existed in the Primitive Church, namely, apostles, prophets, pastors, teachers, evangelists, and so forth.

7 We believe in the gift of tongues, prophecy, revelation, visions, healing, interpretation of tongues, and so forth.

8 We believe the Bible to be the word of God as far as it is translated correctly; we also believe the Book of Mormon to be the word of God.

9 We believe all that God has revealed, all that He does now reveal, and we believe that He will yet reveal many great and important things pertaining to the Kingdom of God.

10 We believe in the literal gathering of Israel and in the restoration of the Ten Tribes; that Zion (the New Jerusalem) will be built upon the American continent; that Christ will reign personally upon the earth; and, that the earth will be renewed and receive its paradisiacal glory.

11 We claim the privilege of worshiping Almighty God according to the dictates of our own conscience, and allow all men the same privilege, let them worship how, where, or what they may.

12 We believe in being subject to kings, presidents, rulers, and magistrates, in obeying, honoring, and sustaining the law.

13 We believe in being honest, true, chaste, benevolent, virtuous, and in doing good to all men; indeed, we may say that we follow the admonition of Paul—We believe all things, we hope all things, we have endured many things, and hope to be able to endure all things. If there is anything virtuous, lovely, or of good report or praiseworthy, we seek after these things.
JOSEPH SMITH

ADDTITIONAL BELIEFS ADDED BY THE AUTHOR

14. We believe in keeping our bodies free from harmful drugs, alcohol. Caffeine, nicotine, or any other habit forming products.
15. We believe that families can be together forever if the marriage is performed by proper authority in an LDS temple.
16. We believe in baptism and other saving ordinances for the dead for all those who die without knowledge of the gospel.
17. We believe in a universal resurrection, a final judgement and assignment to a degree of glory.

SATAN THE DEVIL AND HIS HOSTS ARE REAL: Satan and one third of the hosts of heaven were cast down to the earth to tempt and torment man. Good spirits can help you see the good in life and evil spirits can direct you in the wrong paths.

HOW CAN GOD ANSWER ALL OF OUR PRAYERS AT THE SAME TIME? God is surrounded with the innumerable hosts of heaven, two thirds stayed and one third was cast down with Satan. We may each have a guardian angel assigned to us as depicted in Jimmy Stewart's movie; "It's a Wonderful Life". But remember God is all-powerful and all knowing so he knows how to do it.

I believe God has had a hand in helping inventors invent all of the wonderful things that have been accomplished in communication, transportation, buildings, equipment and internet that has brought us to the point where we are today.

WORLD CONFLICTS AND RELIGION
Religion does play a major role in the cause and effects of the world conflicts now going on. The terrorists groups seem to come from the Islamic religious adherents. They claim that their religion teaches zero tolerance for other religions for everyone must convert to their way or be put to death. There appears to be no compromise with people who have this philosophy so we have to get them before they get us. We cannot accomplish this by pulling out of Iraq and Afghanistan now no matter how we got into it or what we have lost up to this point.

WORLD LEADERS WHO HAVE SOUGHT PROPHETIC GUIDANCE
King David:
And the Lord sent Nathan unto David. And he came unto him, and said unto him, There were two men in one city; the one rich, and the other poor.

The rich man had exceeding many flocks and herds:

But the poor man had nothing, save one little ewe lamb, which he had bought and nourished up: and it grew up together with him, and with his children; it did eat of his own meat, and drank of his own cup, and lay in his bosom, and was unto him as a daughter.

And there came a traveler unto the rich man, and he spared to take of his own flock and of his own herd, to dress for the wayfaring man that was come unto him; but took the poor man's lamb, and dressed it for the man that was come to him.

And David's anger was greatly kindled against the man; and he said to Nathan, As the Lord liveth, the man that hath done this thing shall surely die:

And he shall restore the lamb fourfold, because he did this thing, and because he had no pity.

And Nathan said to David, Thou art the man. Thus saith the Lord God of Israel, I anointed thee king over Israel, and I delivered thee out of the hand of Saul;

And I gave thee thy master's house, and thy master's wives into thy bosom, and gave thee the house of Israel and of Judah; and if that had been too little, I would moreover have given unto thee such and such things.

Wherefore hast thou despised the commandment of the Lord, to do evil in his sight? Thou hast killed Uriah the Hittite with the sword, and hast taken his wife to be thy wife, and hast slain him with the sword of the children of Ammon.

Now therefore the sword shall never depart from thine house; because thou hast despised me, and hast taken the wife of Uriah the Hittite to be thy wife. 2 Samuel 12:1-10

THE BOOK OF MORMON WARS
Moroni is the Chief Captain of the Nephite Army and seeks advice from Alma, the Prophet.
But it came to pass, as soon as they had departed into the wilderness Moroni sent spies into the wilderness to watch their camp; and Moroni, also, knowing of the prophecies of Alma, sent certain men unto him, desiring him that he should inquire of the Lord whither the armies of the Nephites should go to defend themselves against the Lamanites.

And it came to pass that the word of the Lord came unto Alma, and Alma informed the messengers of Moroni, that the armies of the Lamanites were marching round about in the wilderness, that they might come over into the land of Manti, that they might commence an attack upon the weaker part of the people. And those messengers went and delivered the message unto Moroni. Alma 43:23-24

EXAMPLE OF PRAYER

MY FOLKS
When I was four years old my folks were renting a farm one-mile west of the Happy

HAPPY VALLEY SCHOOL

Valley school near Nampa, Idaho. It was early spring and the cheat grass was getting up good among the sage brush and I was helping my mother herd our milk cows while they were getting some of this early grass.

Golden and Nephi

 Two of my older brothers, Nephi 15 and Golden 17 had been harrowing some farmland on this farm with horses hooked to the harrow. They got the idea to just unhook the horses and leave them standing in the field and they ran away from home and hopped a freight train headed for California. My mother was so worried about them, she said, we need to pray for our boys that they will come back safe. So we knelt down by sagebrush and she prayed mightily that the boys would return home without harm or accident.

The boys did return home in a few weeks and told hair-raising stories of how they had gotten separated from each other and didn't know what to do or how to find each other. They said the Lord blessed them to be able to find each other because they were each riding on different trains going in opposite direction when they happened to notice the other one on the other train and were able to trace it.

Golden and Nephi Grigg were the founders of the ORE-IDA FOODS. They started it from a defunct pea packing plant but soon began processing frozen corn on the cob and French fried potatoes and eventually sold out to Heinz Foods as it now is in Ontario, Oregon. They invented the Tater Tot which became a food item in great demand so it was a big factor contributing to the success of the company.

KEEPING THE SABBATH DAY HOLY

COLLEGE OF IDAHO

FARMING LOSS
I was farming a 260 acre rented farm located near the Malheur Butte between Ontario and Vale. I tried my hand at row cropping raising potatoes, sugar beets and grain. I hired a young man neighbor to help me and financed my operation at a local bank. I didn't make enough on the crops to pay the bank so I held a farm auction on my equipment to get the money to pay the bank. I decided to go back to school and finish my education and start teaching high school. So I enrolled for classes at the College of Idaho in Caldwell, Idaho and drove to school from Vale until we could move over to Caldwell.

Malheur butte

KEEPING THE SABBATH DAY HOLY

I checked my schedule and classes with a college advisor and found out that I needed a 3-hour credit in Analytical Geometry in order to complete my major in Business and a minor in math. I was at mid year of my senior college year and I had not even taken regular geometry in high school. So I enrolled in an Analytic Geometry class at about mid term of the school year. When I looked over the textbook I was completely snowed, as I hardly knew head or tales where to start. The professor announced on Friday that we would have a major exam for the course at 8 A.M. Monday. I said to my wife that I consider my schoolwork as my regular job and that I should rest from studies on Sunday to clear my head. I decided to get up at 3 A.M. on Monday and study until 7:30 A.M. then go take the exam. I studied the exercises at the end of each chapter and pretty much memorized them. When I got to school and received a copy of the exam I couldn't believe my eyes because every question was just exactly what I had memorized at home. It just took me few minutes to put the answers down and was the first one to hand my test paper in and everyone looked at me with questionable eyes. I received an A for the course.

This was a great testimony to me of how the Lord can help you when you keep his commandments.

MARRIAGE, ABORTION AND HOMOSEXUALITY

THE EARTH'S PURPOSE

Remember the two thirds of the spirit children that were not cast out with Lucifer to the earth to tempt and torment man. These faithful spirit children would have the privilege of coming to this earth, receive a mortal body and be tried and proven worthy or unworthy to inherit eternal life with God.

Marriage, family life and having babies is the way the Lord set up the process of bringing spirits from heaven to earth. Then death is provided to take people out of this life and back to the God who gave them life. The spirit and body will then be resurrected and face a final judgement and will be assigned an eternal home.

Marriage is ordained of God and blessed by God and is necessary that every capable man and woman partake of it in order to fulfill their purpose for coming to earth. Abortion and homosexuality are practices that thwart Gods' purpose for creating the earth.

I treat my homosexual son and his partner both as my children. I love them but it grieves me that I am robbed of having their children and grandchildren to carry on our family name and be of service to our church and country.

CHAPTER- 2
ECONOMY SKYROCKET AND IMMIGRATION REFORM

PROPOSAL OF HOW TO FREE THE PEOPLE AND MAKE THE ECONOMY SKYROCKET.

Our government is planning to spend billions and trillions of dollars to cut down carbon emissions from the earth besides the billions already spent for space exploration and foreign aid. It is time we look at our own land and it's people who need help. America has been and will continue to be a Land of Promise to those who live here and millions of others around the world who would like to come here and have families and own property and live a free life of many opportunities.

A proposal is in the making by our present administration to set aside millions of acres of land, beautiful timberland and grazing land as a wilderness where vehicles and animals are prohibited. This land will be just to look at like a picture on the wall. There will be no production or anything of value come from it other than looks. When I drive through these areas I see what could be beautiful homes and gardens and fences and animals, poultry and all kinds of livestock, children playing in the yards and many activities going on.

The following ideas are set forth to show what could be done with this land and the projects connected with it to provide needed homes and employment for millions of people who are out work and needing a home but cannot afford to buy one.

A. CITIZENSHIP
1. Repeal the present expensive and time consuming citizenship laws that prevents so many good people from becoming citizens.
2. Reinstate the original law that required only that a person take an Oath of Allegiance denouncing any allegiance to any other country or ruler. This to be free of charge except for the cost of filing.
   a. The person to be positively identified with fingerprints, DNA tests and entered into a national computer database.
   b. The person's criminal history researched and any crimes not satisfied anywhere must be satisfied before citizenship granted.
   c. The person cannot be a member of any criminal gang or anti-American group.
   d. Have a 3-yr. waiting period to prove up but have driving and work privileges.

3. Those aliens that are already here, let them process into citizenship the same as a new comer.

B.   LAND USE LAWS
1.   Revise present Wilderness laws, BLM and Forest Laws that prohibit use of the land for homes and population growth. Cattle, horse and sheep grazing on government lands to be phased out. BLM and Forest Service Agencies to become land sales and settlement offices. National Parks and monuments to stay in tact.
2.   Re-instate the Homestead laws and revise them so as to permit a homestead of one acre outside of a city and a city lot size inside a city.
   a. A charge of $10,000 to $20,000 for a country or city lot that would include water, sewer and road access (At least a gravel road to the property outside the city and a paved road inside the city) (City sewer and water inside a city and well and septic tank outside the city). This cost amortized over a 10 yr. Term with interest at 6% per annum, payments starting one year from date of purchase with a $10. Down payment.
   b. Government survey crews would establish lot and block lines as part of the cost of the lot.
   c. The government to put in roads, sewer and water as part of the cost of the lot would hire developers.
   d. The government to put in electric and phone service as part of the cost of the lot would hire Electric Companies and Phone Companies.

3.   Land would be developed in a systematic and contiguous manner. Each township could have a market center that would be built up by private entrepreneurs assisted by low interest government backing.
   a.   Persons purchasing a lot could obtain a government backed low interest loan to build a home on it.
   b.   Veterans would be given a land grant of a home lot with all utilities and roads in.

4.   Long term-leased land could also be used for development such as state school lands. Land now being leased for grazing at 50 cents or a dollar per acre per year would bring 20 times that for development.

C.   ROAD AND BRIDGE PROJECT
1.   All U.S. Highways to be increased to at least four lanes with freeways in more populated areas and on grade crossings in less populated areas.
2.   Present bridges and roads to be inspected and those replaced that are hazardous.

D.   MAKE HIGH SPEED INTERNET AND TV AVAILABLE TO EVERYONE

E.   HOW TO FINANC\E THESE PROJECTS AND IMPROVEMENTS

1.   We sold war savings bonds to our own people to finance WWII. Why couldn't we sell MAKE AMERICA GREAT savings bonds to finance these projects and pay off foreign creditors?

2.   Make the bonds so that they produce a better return than savings accounts now do and you will get plenty of takers.

F.   EFFECT ON THE ECONOMY

1.   It is hard to estimate the effect on our economy but reason tells me that with all this activity, millions of people would be put to work, millions of people would be able to buy homes and billions of dollars would be pumped into the economy.

CHAPTER 3
EDUCATION, MILITARY AND HOMELAND SECURITY

ELEMENTARY SCHOOLS
Elementary schools to include kindergarten and primary grades plus the regular 8 grades to equal a 10-year course of study.

HIGH SCHOOLS
High Schools to include the first two years of regular college courses for a six-year course of study. National Guard training for all those over 18 in summer and some weekends.

COLLEGES AND UNIVERSITIES
Colleges and Universities to have 4 years of post High School study and include MBAs and Doctoral degrees and comparable degrees in other subjects.

MILITARY
National Guard at home and abroad to replace Home Land Security and provide military protection at transportation terminals on land, sea and air. Military protection at major communication terminals of telephone, telegraph, radio, television and Internet providers. Also all schools from elementary to universities to have military protection. National Guard to work and cooperate with local law enforcement Agencies to provide this military protection with possible sharing of costs.

CHAPTER 4
FOREIGN RELATIONS AND UNITED NATIONS

NO FREEBEES
 If people or countries need help, make them work to pay for it or provide for them to pay it back when able or have them furnish troops or equipment or humanitarian aid to the UN, Red Cross or church organizations who are set up to help.

 Countries like Iraq that is rich in oil should be paying us back for the money and lives spent over there. We shouldn't help people unless they are willing to help themselves when they are able. The same principle should apply as to giving welfare help to individuals and families in this country,

LEND- LEASE
Review the Lend-Lease agreements worked out with a number of countries like Britain, France and Russia during and after WWII. This was a brilliant idea that helped recoup a lot of money spent helping these countries.

PROTECTION AT HOME
A   It seems that our nation has become infested with thieves and thugs to where policemen and juries cannot issue a fair judgement for fear of a riot or personal harm awaiting them in the streets and dark corners. Their numbers are increasing so that soon they will be able to elect thugs and robbers to rule over us. So we must take bold steps to nip this trend while we can. The following is a suggestion on how to do it.

REPLACE THE DEPARTMENT OF HOMELAND SECURITY WITH THE
NATIONAL GUARD

B   THE NATIONAL GUARD WOULD HIRE ALL OF THE
UNEMPLOYED AND THE TERM "UNEMPLOYMENT" WOULD BE HISTORY

Our National Guard would protect all schools, air, sea, and land terminals for transportation of people and goods. As also production plants, sports events, movie theaters, hospitals, clinics, churches and temples.   Any place that a crowd can gather.

Estimate this would increase the Guard strength to about 5 million people.

C How to finance and pay for this protection: Same way that we pay for protection during a shooting war. In this case the war is on thuggism and terrorism. In the world that we live in today we cannot afford to leave anything to chance when it comes to protecting individuals or groups of individuals. This could work in partnership so the Protected businesses or schools pay part of the cost.

D We live in a Free America and it is free also to any crazy person to make explosives and blow us up or to shoot us down.

Instead of paying out all of this unemployment compensation and welfare for nothing, hire these same people with almost the same money to protect us.

E Is this plan possible? Yes

F   What would it do for America? It would give every citizen a feeling of comfort and security and would give everyone a job and livelihood who wants one. It would also help maintain our military strength at home and abroad.

PROTECTION ABROAD AND FOREIGN AID

A.   First of all we need we need to wipe out the International bands of robbers and murderers such as theTalaban, Isis and others. We belong to and pay dues to a world organization set up to do just that but for some reason it is not being done. Here is what the document says:
The Purposes of the United Nations are:
To maintain international peace and security, and to that end: to take effective collective measures for the prevention and removal of threats to the peace, and for the suppression of acts of aggression or other breaches of the peace, and to bring about by peaceful means, and in conformity with the principles of justice and international law, adjustment or settlement of international disputes or situations which might lead to a breach of the peace;

B.   There are 193 National States that belong to the United Nations probably totaling about 6 billion people dedicated to keeping peace on earth. This huge organization is letting a few Talaban and Isis extremists over run war torn Syria and Iraq. The U N could appoint retired military leaders and ask for 1- 2 million volunteers of men, equipment and supplies from all members based on a percentage of population. The U.S. portion would amount to about 5%. 5% of 2 million would be 100,000. This UN peacekeeping army could wipe out the Talaban and Isis and other murderous groups in Iraq and other countries anywhere in the world.

C.   FOREIGN AID
Instead of giving cash for aid I think we could better work out a trade or something like the Lend- Lease program of WWII. Just think of the billions of dollars we poured into Iraq without any obligation on their part to pay us back. I thought that Iraq being one the richest oil producing countries in the world would surely be able to repay us but no, not a cent.

D Our war machine is for our protection and not invasion of other countries. Our motto is to "Speak softly but carry a big stick," Theodore Roosevelt. We will keep our military might superior in the world. We will help make the UN a viable world peacekeeping force and encourage all nations to abide by its principles.

E is this plan possible and compatible with what we want to accomplish? Yes, but we have to get Russia and China to agree to it.

F What would this do for America?   It would help us maintain our wealth. We would be like a big bank. Make loans but get it back with interest. Yes, because we are masters of our own destiny and of our own assets so we can deal fairly.

CHAPTER 5

TAXES, INTEREST AND DEBT

TAXES

I think most everyone realizes that taxes are a necessary evil to pay for government protection and services. When I was making money I didn't mind paying taxes including social security payments.

Right now we are in a period of inflation on goods and services we buy and a period of deflation on most goods we sell. An example: If I were to build a house to sell, when I got it built it would not be worth what it cost to build it. Every day it costs more to build it but the value is not increasing with the cost.

TAX CREDITS: Supply and demand is what causes this situation and the answer is to get the unemployed people back to work such as I outlined in Chapter 2 herein. Tax incentives such as tax credits for investment in equipment and projects to rebuild America are wonderful ways to entice business people to move forward. Everybody wins this way, the government ends up getting more taxes, businesses end up making more money and paying more taxes but they don't mind paying more taxes when they are making money. Schools have more money to expand their services rather than contract them. Interest and savings rates can go up to a decent amount for those who are living on interest. So everyone is happy.

DOESN'T MATTER WHAT WE OWE:

When I was taking a business class in college, the Professor told us that it didn't matter what we owe because the government can set the interest rate so our payments won't increase. This may have been true when we just owed ourselves but now that we owe a large share of our national debt to a foreign power it is no longer true. We need to get our foreign creditors paid off. I think a good way to do this to make and sell our new savings bonds called MAKE AMERICA GREAT in a number of different dimensions and attractive interest rates and our people would shift their savings into these bonds and we could pay off our foreign creditors.

THE FISCAL CLIFF DEBATE: I tried every way to get this message to our congressmen, news media, political committees and no one would listen.

FISCAL CLIFF SOLUTION

And it came to pass in those days, that there went out a decree from Barak Obama, that all the world should be taxed.

Let Obama have his tax increase on the top 2% of the rich but provide for a tax credit of 10 – 15% of investment for the rich investors who are willing to put up money to finance projects to rebuild America such as the infra-structure, transportation, communication, housing and etc. This would likely offset the increased tax rate they would have to pay. This would also accomplish three things, jobs, revenue and lower net taxes for most people. Do not close up the loopholes you are thinking about such as the itemized deductions and the capital gains tax because these really help the middle income tax payers. Thanks and Merry Christmas, Dick Grigg, Ph 541-372-2623, Nyssa, Oregon.

THE END RESULT:

Obama got his way with raising taxes on the top 2% of the rich but we didn't get the tax credits on investments as incentives for people to put up the money to rebuild America. In fact not a word was said about creating jobs and putting the unemployed back to work.

CHAPTER 6

Who is the best shot for our next President?

DONALD JOHN TRUMP

 Born: June 14th, 1946 (age 68)
Donald Trump for President
Donald Trump was born in the neighborhood of Queens in New York City, New York, to parents of German and Scottish descent. He earned academic honors in basic schooling, where he also proved a gifted student athlete, before going on to study first at Fordham University and then at the Wharton School of the University of Pennsylvania. He graduated in 1968, earning a Bachelor of Science degree in Economics.

Trump would go on to become a successful real estate magnate, where his determination and talent for business shone. Despite falling on hard times, challenges within the real estate market causing him to plummet from riches to a depth of destitution that prompted him to declare bankruptcy, he remained an active player in the industry, ultimately rebuilding his empire and earning back his lost fortune. His proclivity for public activity and his success in the public eye, particularly as host of his popular reality show "The Apprentice", have made him a celebrity in the United States.

Never one to shy away from controversy, Trump has toyed with the idea of a Republican or even Independent presidential run on numerous occasions, though to date he has never followed through. He has a tendency to service his image for these potential runs with extravagant public antics, such as his decision in 2011 to join the infamous ranks of nigh-universally conservative Americans who questioned President Barack Obama's birth within the United States. Dubbed "birthers" - in an unflattering and derogatory comparison to the "truther" conspiracy theorists who maintain that the September 11, 2001 terror attacks were orchestrated by the US government – these Americans accused Obama of having actually been born in Kenya, and thus being constitutionally ineligible for the office of President.

Donald Trump Presidential Announcement Speech

Last week, I read 2,300 Humvees— these are big vehicles— were left behind for the enemy. 2,000? You would say maybe two, maybe four? 2,300 sophisticated vehicles, they ran, and the enemy took them.

Last quarter, it was just announced our gross domestic product— a sign of strength, right? But not for us. It was below zero. Whoever heard of this? It's never below zero.

Our labor participation rate was the worst since 1978. But think of it, GDP below zero, horrible labor participation rate.

And our real unemployment is anywhere from 18 to 20 percent. Don't believe the 5.6. Don't believe it. That's right. A lot of people up there can't get jobs. They can't get jobs, because there are no jobs, because China has our jobs and Mexico has our jobs. They all have jobs. But the real number, the real number is anywhere from 18 to 19 and maybe even 21 percent, and nobody talks about it, because it's a statistic that's full of nonsense. Our enemies are getting stronger and stronger by the way, and we as a country are getting weaker. Even our nuclear arsenal doesn't work.

It came out recently they have equipment that is 30 years old. They don't know if it worked. And I thought it was horrible when it was broadcast on television, because boy, does that send signals to Putin and all of the other people that look at us and they say, "That is a group of people, and that is a nation that truly has no clue. They don't know what they're doing. They don't know what they're doing."

We have a disaster called the big lie: Obamacare. Obamacare.
Yesterday, it came out that costs are going for people up 29, 39, 49, and even 55 percent, and deductibles are through the roof. You have to be hit by a tractor, literally, a tractor, to use it, because the deductibles are so high, it's virtually useless. It's virtually useless. It is a disaster.

And remember the $5 billion website? $5 billion we spent on a website, and to this day it doesn't work. A $5 billion website. I have so many websites, I have them all over the place. I hire people, they do a website. It costs me $3. $5 billion website.

Well, you need somebody, because politicians are all talk, no action. Nothing's gonna get done. They will not bring us— believe me— to the promised land. They will not.
As an example, I've been on the circuit making speeches, and I hear my fellow Republicans. And they're wonderful people. I like them. They all want me to support them. They don't know how to bring it about. They come up to my office. I'm meeting with three of them in the next week. And they don't know— "Are you running? Are you not running? Could we have your support? What do we do? How do we do it?"

I like them. And I hear their speeches. And they don't talk jobs and they don't talk China. When was the last time you heard China is killing us? They're devaluing their currency to a level that you wouldn't believe. It makes it impossible for our companies to compete, impossible. They're killing us.

But you don't hear that from anybody else. You don't hear it from anybody else. And I watch the speeches. I watch the speeches of these people, and they say the sun will rise, the moon will set, all sorts of wonderful things will happen. And people are saying, "What's going on? I just want a job. Just get me a job. I don't need the rhetoric. I want a job."

And that's what's happening. And it's going to get worse, because remember, Obamacare really kicks in in '16, 2016. Obama is going to be out playing golf. He might be on one of my courses. I would invite him, I actually would say. I have the best courses in the world, so I'd say, you what, if he wants to— I have one right next to the White House, right on the Potomac. If he'd like to play, that's fine. In fact, I'd love him to leave early and play, that would be a very good thing.

But Obamacare kicks in in 2016. Really big league. It is going to be amazingly destructive. Doctors are quitting. I have a friend who's a doctor, and he said to me the other day, "Donald, I never saw anything like it. I have more accountants than I have nurses. It's a disaster. My patients are beside themselves. They had a plan that was good. They have no plan now."

We have to repeal Obamacare, and it can be— and— and it can be replaced with something much better for everybody. Let it be for everybody. But much better and much less expensive for people and for the government. And we can do it.

So I've watched the politicians. I've dealt with them all my life. If you can't make a good deal with a politician, then there's something wrong with you. You're certainly not very good. And that's what we have representing us. They will never make America great again. They don't even have a chance. They're controlled fully— they're controlled fully by the lobbyists, by the donors, and by the special interests, fully.

Yes, they control them. Hey, I have lobbyists. I have to tell you. I have lobbyists that can produce anything for me. They're great. But you know what? it won't happen. It won't happen. Because we have to stop doing things for some people, but for this country, it's destroying our country. We have to stop, and it has to stop now.

Now, our country needs— our country needs a truly great leader, and we need a truly great leader now. We need a leader that wrote "The Art of the Deal."
We need a leader that can bring back our jobs, can bring back our manufacturing, can bring back our military, can take care of our vets. Our vets have been abandoned.
And we also need a cheerleader.

You know, when President Obama was elected, I said, "Well, the one thing, I think he'll do well. I think he'll be a great cheerleader for the country. I think he'd be a great spirit."

He was vibrant. He was young. I really thought that he would be a great cheerleader. He's not a leader. That's true. You're right about that.

But he wasn't a cheerleader. He's actually a negative force. He's been a negative force. He wasn't a cheerleader; he was the opposite.

We need somebody that can take the brand of the United States and make it great again. It's not great again. We need— we need somebody— we need somebody that literally will take this country and make it great again. We can do that.

And, I will tell you, I love my life. I have a wonderful family. They're saying, "Dad, you're going to do something that's going to be so tough."You know, all of my life, I've heard that a truly successful person, a really, really successful person and even modestly successful cannot run for public office. Just can't happen. And yet that's the kind of mindset that you need to make this country great again.

So ladies and gentlemen…I am officially running… for president of the United States, and we are going to make our country great again.

It can happen. Our country has tremendous potential. We have tremendous people.

We have people that aren't working. We have people that have no incentive to work. But they're going to have incentive to work, because the greatest social program is a job. And they'll be proud, and they'll love it, and they'll make much more than they would've ever made, and they'll be— they'll be doing so well, and we're going to be thriving as a country, thriving. It can happen.

I will be the greatest jobs president that God ever created. I tell you that.

I'll bring back our jobs from China, from Mexico, from Japan, from so many places. I'll bring back our jobs, and I'll bring back our money.

Right now, think of this: We owe China $1.3 trillion. We owe Japan more than that. So they come in, they take our jobs, they take our money, and then they loan us back the money, and we pay them in interest, and then the dollar goes up so their deal's even better.

How stupid are our leaders? How stupid are these politicians to allow this to happen? How stupid are they? I'm going to tell you— thank you. I'm going to tell you a couple of stories about trade, because I'm totally against the trade bill for a number of reasons.

Number one, the people negotiating don't have a clue. Our president doesn't have a clue. It is a done deal. It's going in and that's going to be it, going into Tennessee. Great state, great people.

All of a sudden, at the last moment, this big car manufacturer, foreign, announces they're not going to Tennessee. They're gonna spend their $1 billion in Mexico instead. Not good. Now, Ford announces a few weeks ago that Ford is going to build a $2.5 billion car and truck and parts manufacturing plant in Mexico. $2.5 billion, it's going to be one of the largest in the world. Ford. Good company.

So I announced that I'm running for president. I would...... one of the early things I would do, probably before I even got in— and I wouldn't even use— you know, I have— I know the smartest negotiators in the world. I know the good ones. I know the bad ones. I know the overrated ones. You get a lot of them that are overrated. They're not good. They think they are. They get good stories, because the newspapers get buffaloed. But they're not good.

But I know the negotiators in the world, and I put them one for each country. Believe me, folks. We will do very, very well, very, very well. But I wouldn't even waste my time with this one. I would call up the head of Ford, who I know. If I was president, I'd say, "Congratulations. I understand that you're building a nice $2.5 billion car factory in Mexico and that you're going to take your cars and sell them to the United States zero tax, just flow them across the border."

And you say to yourself, "How does that help us," right? "How does that help us? Where is that good"? It's not. So I would say, "Congratulations. That's the good news. Let me give you the bad news. Every car and every truck and every part manufactured in this plant that comes across the border, we're going to charge you a 35-percent tax, and that tax is going to be paid simultaneously with the transaction, and that's it."

Now, here's what is going to happen. If it's not me in the position, it's one of these politicians that we're running against, you know, the 400 people that we're (inaudible). And here's what's going to happen. They're not so stupid. They know it's not a good thing, and they may even be upset by it. But then they're going to get a call from the donors or probably from the lobbyist for Ford and say, "You can't do that to Ford, because Ford takes care of me and I take care of you, and you can't do that to Ford."

And guess what? No problem. They're going to build in Mexico. They're going to take away thousands of jobs. It's very bad for us. So under President Trump, here's what would happen: The head of And by the way, I'm not even saying that's the kind of mindset, that's the kind of thinking you need for this country.

So— because we got to make the country rich. It sounds crass. Somebody said, "Oh, that's crass." It's not crass. Ford will call me back, I would say within an hour after I told them the bad news. But it could be he'd want to be cool, and he'll wait until the next day. You know, they want to be a little cool. And he'll say, "Please, please, please." He'll beg for a little while, and I'll say, "No interest." Then he'll call all sorts of political people, and I'll say, "Sorry, fellas. No interest," because I don't need anybody's money. It's nice. I don't need anybody's money. I'm using my own money. I'm not using the lobbyists. I'm not using donors. I don't care. I'm really rich. I (inaudible). He's a bad negotiator.

He's the one that did Bergdahl. We get Bergdahl, they get five killer terrorists that everybody wanted over there. We get Bergdahl. We get a traitor. We get a no-good traitor, and they get the five people that they wanted for years, and those people are now back on the battlefield trying to kill us. That's the negotiator we have.

Take a look at the deal he's making with Iran. He makes that deal, Israel maybe won't exist very long. It's a disaster, and we have to protect Israel. But…

So we need people— I'm a free trader. But the problem with free trade is you need really talented people to negotiate for you. If you don't have talented people, if you don't have great leadership, if you don't have people that know business, not just a political hack that got the job because he made a contribution to a campaign, which is the way all jobs, just about, are gotten, free trade terrible.

Free trade can be wonderful if you have smart people, but we have people that are stupid. We have people that aren't smart. And we have people that are controlled by special interests. And it's just not going to work.
\
So, here's a couple of stories happened recently. A friend of mine is a great manufacturer. And, you know, China comes over and they dump all their stuff, and I buy it. I buy it, because, frankly, I have an obligation to buy it, because they devalue their currency so brilliantly, they just did it recently, and nobody thought they could do it again.

But with all our problems with Russia, with all our problems with everything— everything, they got away with it again. And it's impossible for our people here to compete.

So I want to tell you this story. A friend of mine who's a great manufacturer, calls me up a few weeks ago. He's very upset. I said, "What's your problem?"

He said, "You know, I make great product."

And I said, "I know. I know that because I buy the product."

He said, "I can't get it into China. They won't accept it. I sent a boat over and they actually sent it back. They talked about environmental, they talked about all sorts of crap that had nothing to do with it."

I said, "Oh, wait a minute, that's terrible. Does anyone know this?"

He said, "Yeah, they do it all the time with other people."

I said, "They send it back?"

"Yeah. So I finally got it over there and they charged me a big tariff. They're not supposed to be doing that. I told them."

Now, they do charge you tariff on trucks, when we send trucks and other things over there.

Ask Boeing. They wanted Boeing's secrets. They wanted their patents and all their secrets before they agreed to buy planes from Boeing.

Hey, I'm not saying they're stupid. I like China. I sell apartments for— I just sold an apartment for $15 million to somebody from China. Am I supposed to dislike them? I own a big chunk of the Bank of America Building at 1290 Avenue of the Americas, that I got from China in a war. Very valuable.

I love China. The biggest bank in the world is from China. You know where their United States headquarters is located? In this building, in Trump Tower. I love China. People say, "Oh, you don't like China?"

No, I love them. But their leaders are much smarter than our leaders, and we can't sustain ourselves with that. There's too much— it's like— it's like take the New England Patriots and Tom Brady and have them play your high school football team. That's the difference between China's leaders and our leaders.

They are ripping us. We are rebuilding China. We're rebuilding many countries. China, you go there now, roads, bridges, schools, you never saw anything like it. They have bridges that make the George Washington Bridge look like small potatoes. And they're all over the place.

We have all the cards, but we don't know how to use them. We don't even know that we have the cards, because our leaders don't understand the game. We could turn off that spigot by charging them tax until they behave properly.

Now they're going militarily. They're building a military island in the middle of the South China Sea. A military island. Now, our country could never do that because we'd have to get environmental clearance, and the environmentalist wouldn't let our country— we would never build in an ocean. They built it in about one year, this massive military port.

They're building up their military to a point that is very scary. You have a problem with ISIS. You have a bigger problem with China.

And, in my opinion, the new China, believe it or not, in terms of trade, is Mexico.

So this man tells me about the manufacturing. I say, "That's a terrible story. I hate to hear it." But I have another one, Ford.

So Mexico takes a company, a car company that was going to build in Tennessee, rips it out. Everybody thought the deal was dead. Reported it in the Wall Street Journal recently. Everybody thought it was dead.

Yes, Donald Trump Is Running for President
Yes, Donald Trump Is Running for President

14 Presidential Candidates Ranked by Their Net worth Promoted
14 Presidential Candidates Ranked by Their Net Worth
Wow. Whoa. That is some group of people. Thousands.

So nice, thank you very much. That's really nice. Thank you. It's great to be at Trump Tower. It's great to be in a wonderful city, New York. And it's an honor to have everybody here. This is beyond anybody's expectations. There's been no crowd like this.

And, I can tell, some of the candidates, they went in. They didn't know the air-conditioner didn't work. They sweated like dogs.

They didn't know the room was too big, because they didn't have anybody there. How are they going to beat ISIS? I don't think it's gonna happen.

Our country is in serious trouble. We don't have victories anymore. We used to have victories, but we don't have them. When was the last time anybody saw us beating, let's say, China in a trade deal? They kill us. I beat China all the time. All the time.

When did we beat Japan at anything? They send their cars over by the millions, and what do we do? When was the last time you saw a Chevrolet in Tokyo? It doesn't exist, folks. They beat us all the time.

When do we beat Mexico at the border? They're laughing at us, at our stupidity. And now they are beating us economically. They are not our friends, believe me. But they're killing us economically.

The U.S. has become a dumping ground for everybody else's problems.

Thank you. It's true, and these are the best and the finest. When Mexico sends its people, they're not sending their best. They're not sending you. They're not sending you. They're sending people that have lots of problems, and they're bringing those problems with us. They're bringing drugs. They're bringing crime. They're rapists. And some, I assume, are good people.

But I speak to border guards and they tell us what we're getting. And it only makes common sense. It only makes common sense. They're sending us not the right people. It's coming from more than Mexico. It's coming from all over South and Latin America, and it's coming probably— probably— from the Middle East. But we don't know. Because we have no protection and we have no competence, we don't know what's happening. And it's got to stop and it's got to stop fast.

Islamic terrorism is eating up large portions of the Middle East. They've become rich. I'm in competition with them.
They just built a hotel in Syria. Can you believe this? They built a hotel. When I have to build a hotel, I pay interest. They don't have to pay interest, because they took the oil that, when we left Iraq, I said we should've taken.

So now ISIS has the oil, and what they don't have, Iran has. And in 19— and I will tell you this, and I said it very strongly, years ago, I said— and I love the military, and I want to have the strongest military that we've ever had, and we need it more now than ever. But I said, "Don't hit Iraq," because you're going to totally destabilize the Middle East. Iran is going to take over the Middle East, Iran and somebody else will get the oil, and it turned out that Iran is now taking over Iraq. Think of it. Iran is taking over Iraq, and they're taking it over big league.

We spent $2 trillion in Iraq, $2 trillion. We lost thousands of lives, thousands in Iraq. We have wounded soldiers, who I love, I love — they're great — all over the place, thousands and thousands of wounded soldiers.

And we have nothing. We can't even go there. We have nothing. And every time we give Iraq equipment, the first time a bullet goes off in the air, they leave it.

Our enemies are getting stronger and stronger by the way, and we as a country are getting weaker. Even our nuclear arsenal doesn't work.

It came out recently they have equipment that is 30 years old. They don't know if it worked. And I thought it was horrible when it was broadcast on television, because boy, does that send signals to Putin and all of the other people that look at us and they say, "That is a group of people, and that is a nation that truly has no clue. They don't know what they're doing. They don't know what they're doing."

Well, you need somebody, because politicians are all talk, no action. Nothing's gonna get done. They will not bring us— believe me— to the Promised Land. They will not.

As an example, I've been on the circuit making speeches, and I hear my fellow Republicans. And they're wonderful people. I like them. They all want me to support them. They don't know how to bring it about. They come up to my office. I'm meeting with three of them in the next week. And they don't know— "Are you running? Are you not running? Could we have your support? What do we do? How do we do it?" I like them. And I hear their speeches. And they don't talk jobs and they don't talk China. When was the last time you heard China is killing us? They're devaluing their currency to a level that you wouldn't believe. It makes it impossible for our companies to compete, impossible. They're killing us.

But you don't hear that from anybody else. You don't hear it from anybody else. And I watch the speeches.

I watch the speeches of these people, and they say the sun will rise, the moon will set, all sorts of wonderful things will happen. And people are saying, "What's going on? I just want a job. Just get me a job. I don't need the rhetoric. I want a job."

And that's what's happening. And it's going to get worse, because remember, Obamacare really kicks in in '16, 2016. Obama is going to be out playing golf. He might be on one of my courses. I would invite him, I actually would say. I have the best courses in the world, so I'd say, you what, if he wants to— I have one right next to the White House, right on the Potomac. If he'd like to play, that's fine.

In fact, I'd love him to leave early and play, that would be a very good thing.

But Obamacare kicks in in 2016. Really big league. It is going to be amazingly destructive. Doctors are quitting. I have a friend who's a doctor, and he said to me the other day, "Donald, I never saw anything like it. I have more accountants than I have nurses. It's a disaster. My patients are beside themselves. They had a plan that was good. They have no plan now."

We have to repeal Obamacare, and it can be— and— and it can be replaced with something much better for everybody. Let it be for everybody. But much better and much less expensive for people and for the government. And we can do it.
\
So I've watched the politicians. I've dealt with them all my life. If you can't make a good deal with a politician, then there's something wrong with you. You're certainly not very good. And that's what we have representing us. They will never make America great again. They don't even have a chance. They're controlled fully— they're controlled fully by the lobbyists, by the donors, and by the special interests, fully.

Yes, they control them. Hey, I have lobbyists. I have to tell you. I have lobbyists that can produce anything for me. They're great. But you know what? it won't happen. It won't happen. Because we have to stop doing things for some people, but for this country, it's destroying our country. We have to stop, and it has to stop now.

Now, our country needs— our country needs a truly great leader, and we need a truly great leader now. We need a leader that wrote "The Art of the Deal."

We need a leader that can bring back our jobs, can bring back our manufacturing, can bring back our military, can take care of our vets. Our vets have been abandoned.
And we also need a cheerleader. You know, when President Obama was elected, I said, "Well, the one thing, I think he'll do well. I think he'll be a great cheerleader for the country. I think he'd be a great spirit."

He was vibrant. He was young. I really thought that he would be a great cheerleader. He's not a leader. That's true. You're right about that.

But he wasn't a cheerleader. He's actually a negative force. He's been a negative force. He wasn't a cheerleader; he was the opposite.

We need somebody that can take the brand of the United States and make it great again. It's not great again.

We need— we need somebody— we need somebody that literally will take this country and make it great again. We can do that.

And, I will tell you, I love my life. I have a wonderful family. They're saying, "Dad, you're going to do something that's going to be so tough."

You know, all of my life, I've heard that a truly successful person, a really, really successful person and even modestly successful cannot run for public office. Just can't happen. And yet that's the kind of mindset that you need to make this country great again.

So ladies and gentlemen…I am officially running… for president of the United States, and we are going to make our country great again. It can happen. Our country has tremendous potential. We have tremendous people. We have people that aren't working. We have people that have no incentive to work. But they're going to have incentive to work, because the greatest social program is a job. And they'll be proud, and they'll love it, and they'll make much more than they would've ever made, and they'll be— they'll be doing so well, and we're going to be thriving as a country, thriving. It can happen.

I will be the greatest jobs president that God ever created. I tell you that.
I'll bring back our jobs from China, from Mexico, from Japan, from so many places. I'll bring back our jobs, and I'll bring back our money.

Right now, think of this: We owe China $1.3 trillion. We owe Japan more than that. So they come in, they take our jobs, they take our money, and then they loan us back the money, and we pay them in interest, and then the dollar goes up so their deal's even better.

How stupid are our leaders? How stupid are these politicians to allow this to happen? How stupid are they?

I'm going to tell you— thank you. I'm going to tell you a couple of stories about trade, because I'm totally against the trade bill for a number of reasons.
Rebuild the country's infrastructure.
Nobody can do that like me. Believe me. It will be done on time, on budget, way below cost, way below what anyone ever thought.

I look at the roads being built all over the country, and I say I can build those things for one-third. What they do is unbelievable, how bad.

You know, we're building on Pennsylvania Avenue, the Old Post Office, we're converting it into one of the world's great hotels. It's gonna be the best hotel in Washington, D.C. We got it from the General Services Administration in Washington. The Obama administration. We got it. It was the most highly sought after— or one of them, but I think the most highly sought after project in the history of General Services. We got it. People were shocked, Trump got it.

Well, I got it for two reasons. Number one, we're really good. Number two, we had a really good plan. And I'll add in the third, we had a great financial statement. Because the General Services, who are terrific people, by the way, and talented people, they wanted to do a great job. And they wanted to make sure it got built.

So we have to rebuild our infrastructure, our bridges, our roadways, our airports. You come into La Guardia Airport, it's like we're in a third world country. You look at the patches and the 40-year-old floor. They throw down asphalt, and they throw.

You look at these airports, we are like a third world country. And I come in from China and I come in from Qatar and I come in from different places, and they have the most incredible airports in the world. You come to back to this country and you have LAX, disaster. You have all of these disastrous airports. We have to rebuild our infrastructure.

Save Medicare, Medicaid and Social Security without cuts. Have to do it.

Get rid of the fraud. Get rid of the waste and abuse, but save it. People have been paying it for years. And now many of these candidates want to cut it. You save it by making the United States, by making us rich again, by taking back all of the money that's being lost.

Renegotiate our foreign trade deals.

Reduce our $18 trillion in debt, because, believe me, we're in a bubble. We have artificially low interest rates. We have a stock market that, frankly, has been good to me, but I still hate to see what's happening. We have a stock market that is so bloated.

Be careful of a bubble because what you've seen in the past might be small potatoes compared to what happens. So be very, very careful.

And strengthen our military and take care of our vets. So, so important.

Sadly, the American dream is dead.

But if I get elected president I will bring it back bigger and better and stronger than ever before, and we will make America great again.

Thank you. Thank you very much.

SUMMARY

Each of the programs that I have suggested I have shown how it could be put into effect and what it would do for our country. I feel that Trump will come the closest of any of the candidates running for getting the job done.

www.ingramcontent.com/pod-product-compliance
Lightning Source LLC
Chambersburg PA
CBHW080934290526
45795CB00007BA/2748